Blankness, Melancholy, and Other Ways of Dying

Blankness, Melancholy, and Other Ways of Dying

Brenna Lemieux

Five Oaks Press
FIVE-OAKS-PRESS.COM

Copyright ©2017 Brenna Lemieux
All rights reserved. First print edition.

Five Oaks Press
Newburgh, NY 12550
five-oaks-press.com
editor@five-oaks-press.com

ISBN: 978-1-944355-26-5

Cover Art: Kate Weinberg (http://kateweinberg.daportfolio.com/)

Printed in the United States of America

ACKNOWLEDGMENTS

Naugatuck River Review:
"On Mending"

North American Review:
"The Farmer's Tale"

Potomac Review:
"In His Absence, Mr. Huxley Is Unfairly Maligned"

River Styx:
"On Forgery"

*For the sick, the friendless, and the needy,
and for those who are alone*

CONTENTS

In His Absence, Mr. Huxley Is Unfairly Maligned
7

The Farmer's Tale
9

Directions
10

In the Time before Saltshakers
14

On Mending
15

Meanwhile, Next Door
17

On Forgery
19

Terror Incognita
21

Before the Refinement of Suture
23

Aubade: Scratching
24

Courting
25

Once Upon a Time
27

Mowing
28

On Fading
30

Second Puberty
31

Trespassing
33

Dead End
34

Annette Is Fraying
36

On Empty
37

Carl's Life Flashes before His Tongue
38

In His Absence, Mr. Huxley Is Unfairly Maligned

The steam-fingered burnt-popcorn
stench groping her kitchen walls stirs something
long dormant in Mrs. Huxley.

She skims her hands on her hips, slips
into a nightie, pictures Mr. Huxley's lips
when she greets him bare-armed.

He calls to report a delayed flight.
Resolved to wait up, she splits
a book, sips wine, lets the fumes slink closer.

A doze: heat shimmering between her thighs,
skin at a full humping boil, she sweats
through a dream in which her husband,

three stories tall, douses their blazing mattress—
she tries with her simmering
tongue to say, *Stop, stop*, but he sloshes

water from his floppy hose, drenching her,
waves rising around the bed. He's large enough
to pluck her like an ear

of corn from the serving platter, peel her
charred-husk clothes, rub her top to bottom
in butter and devour her—

though knowing him, she dream-thinks,
he's not even hungry.
                            Meantime,
he comes in quietly, hangs his coat, stands

watching his silk-haired wife sleep,
wishing he knew a kernel of her dreams,
how he might wake her gently

to tongue the valley of her spine,
pass his blood-flame to her until she moaned
that her skin would explode

with it, until they erupted
into the salty, soft-edged people
they both thought they had married.

The Farmer's Tale

Jed takes a job reading radio news
to hide the pitchfork lodged in his spine,
can even forget it for stretches
in the dark quiet speaking into the mic
until he steps outside and heads swivel,
hands clap over gasps and the tines sear
again like hot pokers in his discs, sharp
as the morning his brother tripped
in the haymow, lost his grip,
dropped it—sharp as when it first gored.

(When he finally saw the doctor:
Be glad you didn't lose a leg, boy.
Be glad it didn't blind you.)

After a time, Jed takes a wife, a sweet thing
raised in town who never held a fork
bigger than the one she sets on his napkin.
She listens to his radio voice, scrubs
their small house, irons his hole-backed shirts.
Sleeps light as a reed basket while Jed lies
on his stomach, anxious of rolling
in his sleep, of the pitchfork shaft thwacking
her china ribs. The droop of his eyes
worries her and she buys sandpaper,
sits behind him on the sofa and scours
the wooden handle each evening while he reads
her the paper. She says that in time
it will shrink to the size of a doorknob
but privately, she hopes only to smooth it,
to someday come away from loving him
without a crop of splinters in her wrists.

Directions

You are six. Your father drinks too hard, trips
      down the stairs, breaks his neck.
Your mother says you are lost,
      you are both lost. You draw a map.

        Bathroom, kitchen, bedrooms.
    Half squares for the hall stairs.
        Your mother crawls into bed.

You map-label books on shelves, jars
in the medicine chest. Find them
shuffled come morning.
          You revise,

note the soap's shape, the hairs in the drain.
It muddles so you start fresh,
      now that the church ladies
have taken his boots and coat—

but the kitchen sink keeps cluttering.
Your shirt drawer empties and doesn't refill.

You ask when's dinner but she keeps rocking.
You're tired and your feet knock a table,
      smash the family portrait. It's ages

      till she comes over, pinches the
shards from the rug. You watch frozen

    as the edges bite her palm. She closes
her fist around them. She doesn't hear you
      ask for milk.
    She doesn't always wake up.

You pack peanut butter crackers for lunch,
eat the same for supper. Remap

the kitchen, wake up there,
        don't remember sleeping.
Too dark to find the way to your bedroom,
            and something scratches
            the counter behind you.
You wish wish wish you could sleep again—
        then it's morning,

she's up, floating around you. The smell
of eggs frying
      and you're silly Silas, sleepy Silas,
       and she smells soap-and-powder, nuzzles your hair,
presses you
to put on clean clothes.

In the drawer, all your shirts
        fresh and folded. You map.

You map the clean after-school house
and next time she doesn't get up,
     you show it to her.
           She turns to the wall.
           You see the lines
   are smudged, the handwriting poor.
You tear it

and start over, find a ruler, look up rooms
in the dictionary.
          Not enough space

     so you make a series of maps:
     the big one with every room,
     then smaller room-by-room maps,
     then even smaller:
          the silverware drawer,
          the cabinet below the sink.

        You map steak knives and bleach,

map the bathtub, matchbook, razor,
medicine chest.
You map the pillow
in your room,
your mother's bed,
her window,
the laundry line,

empty kitchen cupboards,
stove burners.
You step
into the hall and map the jagged stairs.

You live to map your eighteenth birthday,
but your mother does not.
You are never lost.
You have never left this city.
You walk everywhere
you don't take a bike or bus,
everywhere you don't drive
your taxi.
You know all the shortcuts.

Then it starts again:
the city falls down
a flight of stairs: a flood surges,
a tornado, a fire. Take your pick.
You survive—

you have a gift for living—but you must leave,
find a small town
not submerged or rubbled or charred.
A place you can afford rent.

You buy a train ticket and a map
to study while you wait. A teary young woman approaches,
asks if maps
for you are a foreign tongue,
and if not,

> will you translate for her,
> help her conjugate
> north and east, help her plot
> her way to a room for rent,

> and what can you say but yes,
> what can you do but help heft
her luggage onto the overhead racks?

What can you do but listen to her pour
> her house-uprooted-parents-killed
> into your ear, the weight
> of the atlas settling on your shoulders.

In the Time Before Saltshakers

Sigmund wakes one day with holes
through his thumbs. Clean, nickel-sized,
painless, but with half his pinch gone,

he can't grip cellar salt. Food tastes
dull as scuffed boots. He tries
to plug them with dough, which draws flies,

then clay, which dries and flakes. Chicken
bones warp, rags fray. At supper,
his wife and children sift salt

over mounds of stewed squash, beets, corn.
What flavor, the oldest says, heaping
salt on his third slice of ham,

and the baby claps for the mash
in its sparse-toothed mouth. But that's not
the worst of it. Once flavor ebbs,

color and sound follow: hills level,
lights dim. His wife speaks, his children
speak, and Sigmund hears the drone

of a chronic wind. Through the blur
of tilling, plowing, milking, he feels
neither the sun's hearthstone warmth

nor the seared red throes of fever,
which is what kills him—and even death
he hardly notices except

as a slight negation, a blunt
suction, his whole body slacking
and wreathing into a round, saltless hole.

On Mending

Fred unclips his shirt from the line
to find it has no buttons. He frowns:
last night's wind, twigs whipping

the window screen. He pictures it
pecking thread from the button's eyes,
shivers. Hurries inside.

Because it is his Monday shirt,
he wears it, open, wind clawing
at his chest, tails snapping behind him.

The strange thing, though,
                    is what happens next:
months pass, two dozen unbuttoned Mondays,
and Fred, walking home one night, spies a sapling

sprouting east of his yard. He bends to it:
enamel blossoms, round and flat with pinprick
holes, cottony leaves, deep-woven veins.

He thinks of the word *progeny*, of *manna*,
of the proofs that a person should trust
in the Lord, and snaps a young twig

for his vase. When the buds ripen,
he plucks them, stitches them by lamplight
to his Monday shirt, a neat button hedge.

He tugs, nods, hangs the shirt in his closet.
All fall, wind blusters his clothes,
which he mends tatter by tatter.

When the first snow drops, his shirts'
fibers are completely different than they were
a year ago, just as Fred's own skin has no cell

in common with the skin he wore at birth.
But no one notices, least of all Fred,
whose fingers have grown nimble in time

with the wind's in a liturgy of shredding
and patching his wardrobe, the needle
crossing itself again and again with thread,
the sky knelt down to frost.

Meanwhile, Next Door

At first, Clyde loses just one buttonhole.
Then two more vanish and by Thursday
he can't fasten his shirt. He curses,

glues it shut, rushes to the shop. It unsticks
by lunch and he calls Denise, who says
she never in all her born years.

The larger holes flee next: neck, arm, leg.
His socks like limp boomerangs, boxers
like gutted pillows. Even a steak knife

won't split the cloth, which merges like water
behind the blade. He scans the phonebook
but no one sells holes, calls in naked and loses

his job. Denise brings new pants, but they fuse
at his touch. *Oh dear*, she says, and lifts
the phone. Channel Six agrees to run

an exclusive at ten, and by Monday, donations
arrive: a church group's donut holes, paper
towel roll holes, dog-holes dug in the yard.

Clyde trims and sews them to his shirts, pants,
coat, to the heel of his favorite sock,
right where one used to be. Denise swings by

with takeout and he slaps a hole on the box.
He watches her eat, thinks of all the holes
he takes for granted: doorways and mugs,

the bathtub, pants cuffs and mittens,
her salty wavelet mouth. She wipes her hands
and picks through the heap of holes

beside them, says, *Thank goodness*

for the kindness of strangers, and Clyde agrees.
This is how people go crazy

and propose, he sees, this feeling
that the best thing a person could ever give you
is an absence for you to fill.

On Forgery

Her father, tabling the evening paper,
makes clear he *won't say no again*
and her mother's eyes warn *don't push*,

so Francie decides she'll make a pet instead:
paperclip ribs, old-pantyhose innards, skin
from a widowed glove. Cobweb fur,

thumbtack eyes. She sneaks it milk,
hums to it before bed, snips and pastes
in the quiet bean-soak hours,

before her father's whiskey-voice mushrooms
through the house and her mother re-plugs
the phone so he can roar at everyone

who calls to *wring us dry* (feathers
from a torn coat, wing of a saved
party-drink umbrella)—

soon, she thinks, the creature will stir.
It will nudge her awake, nod her onto its back
and fly her to its family, hundreds

of the motley wild chewing honeysuckle
and dozing in pine-straw nests.
She'll teach them table manners,

how to tiptoe, and won't yell if they chew
too loud or wet the bed. She'll let them
try on her shoes. But after school one day,

she darts upstairs and finds her creature
gone—mistaken for junk, thrown out—
and feels ragged as a ripped sleeve.

She climbs into her mother's lap
and her mother smoothes her hair,
threads a needle and draws it

through Francie's waist, sings *hush little baby*
while she mends the torn place. Soon,
she thinks, Francie will leave her and maybe

she'll follow. They'll find a city apartment
with eccentric neighbors and no roaches,
get jobs and modern haircuts, sigh into

armchairs after work. They'll spend money
on gouda and café meals and fresh jonquils
for the table. They'll listen to jazz at night

and if they have a telephone at all,
they'll keep their number unlisted.

Terror Incognita

She screams at night,
        shrill watery shrieks that slit
the neighbors' eyes when you pass them.

Betty, you say, gripping her arm, *Wake up*,
      until she shudders free,
        sweaty and cow-eyed.

                I'm so sorry,
                she breathes,
                hand at her chest.

You offer water, cold-foot to the kitchen
and when you return
                she's skimmed into sleep.

You climb in and lie wired,
blood glugging your temples, the scream
still kneading your pulse.

What do you dream,
                you ask one morning, bleary
        over toast, almost late for your shift.

Her neck
blushes. She says,
        Nothing. Closes the tap.
Something trying to kill me, is all,
she says. *Stupid*.

        Something? you say,
                      and she says,

Someone. Plucks milk from the icebox,
        tops her coffee.
                      You.

                                          And you chew
your toast, though your mouth's gone
sawdust. You thought you'd hid it better,
thought you'd done the right thing—

                those days after the cyclone,
                folks unhinged, fleeing the city's wreckage—

and out here, you couldn't just leave,
didn't want her to be ruined.
                To have ruined her.
                The neighbors notice.

She is a nice girl, you know that. But now,
        lips greased with butter,
        you see how thick you've been,
        how you're only just peering

into the abyss that was your mistake
in marrying, only just tipping over its edge—

                it's real, what crochets
                her nerves at night.
You have never for a minute loved her.

Before the Refinement of Suture

Arms spread, feet askew on the pedals,
Anne bumps, pitches—
                          street. Chin split.

Gravel, glass, tire-rubber where skin
used to be—
                      blink—
an ER doctor threading a needle.

I see you're prone to a loose face, says his
train-track voice while he dunks her
in Novocain. *I'll just take in these seams*—
a Morse code of pressure along her skull,
                                then velvet.

Pain flames her awake. Spider-leg stitches
ring her face—jaw, ears, hairline—violet
bruises. She's latched so tightly she can't
smile or frown, can't budge her eyebrows,
can't stop her lips hinging apart.

Through her squint-stretched eyelids,
the world's edges shrug out of focus,
but Anne knows she'll never have such
freedom—she's been stitched together
crudely, cartoonishly, sealed tight
as luggage bound for the next world.

Aubade: Scratching

Enid wakes to palms so itchy she could grab
a bouquet of knives blade-first. She opens
the shower tap, frowns at her mirrored thighs:
as if years of scratching have worn her skin
beyond pinning her arms to the bones,
her stomach under the ribs. The students

wear it tighter every fall, and the new
teachers aren't much better, faces so taut
you wonder where the veins fit. Nothing
droops or hints at droop—even the fat ones
glow. She savors the washcloth's bite. Five
in the morning, and she'll just have time

to paint and style and zip herself into a person.
Into the person who drinks coffee by the bucket
and keeps pace even when her skin drags
the way her German Shepherd's paws did
one long-ago trip home from the beach—
her father drove a mile before it clicked:

the burnt-skin asphalt smell, the dog's hind
legs scrambling on the seat—brakes,
Enid helped him inside, thumbed his hot,
grated pads. He didn't bark or whine,
just slept, his feet in her hands until the heat
faded, and the car toiled on, its seats cracked
and sagging, the road scratching bald its tires.

Courting

Maggie wants to look perfect
for her date with Stan
        she buys exfoliating lotion
          she sits on the bathtub's lip she globs she rubs
skin shaves off like caster sugar
sifts into piles the bottle says scrub until skin
        stops peeling she kneads it into her feet
        the heel bone stabs through
        she moves on to the toes
              oh dear she thinks
I should have done this years ago
        her date is in five hours four hours three the pile
            grows below her she can see her tarsals
            metatarsals synovial hinge joint
she doesn't think her shoes match bone she keeps rubbing
        she can always wear black she rubs her calves
        her shin skin the skin around her
            knees thighs stomach

not her chest she needs padding at her chest rubs the lotion
        on her neck arms scalp face the bottle
        says avoid the lips it runs out she scrapes
              the last flakes from her brows
she just has time to shower she towels off
        elbows into her dress twirls squints

frowns her bones aren't white enough she grabs bleach
        buffs off the worst stains Stan rings the bell
        she clatters downstairs
                carpals clicking the banister she swings
back the door tosses her hair
        he looks at her tilts his head you look different
            he says she would blush if she still had skin
            he noticed he cares

            did you get a haircut or something he asks
        she leans to kiss him he turns to the car she tilts

                    forward teeters crack-lands on the pavement
he turns to watch her stand she dusts pebbles from her ulna
            there is no blood
                        don't worry she says no blood
she trips to the car door hooks her fingers under the handle
        it's locked she looks in at Stan wants to tap
        the window he starts the engine
        adjusts the stereo
                    checks the heat she doesn't want
to trouble him
        waits waits waits he looks up opens the door
        I know he says I know what's different
                his phone buzzes the engine scratches

he guesses her necklace
        her heart dumps

there must be another woman she thinks
        he must hate my clothes shoes teeth
        bones hair voice breath

Once Upon a Time

His ghost haunts her tidy house, scans its store
of maps, ignores her. (*Ignores* her—no moan
or wail, no hovering by the bed!) She bakes

bread and he wafts in, floats past attic-bound
sponging up its scent with his dank vapor.
Entire rooms he swells to fill—impossible

to pinpoint.
              She wakes in a lurch, sees him
beside her. Alive. Snoring. No such thing
as ghosts. She tiptoes to the stoop to smoke—

humid tonight, concrete clamming her feet
a familiar, bone-numb chill: loneliness.
It writhes off her skin like steam, fogs

by the clothesline. Persistent. Undeflatable.
The kind of weather pattern no small-town
congregation of rooftops could puncture.

Mowing

Walter's wife calls from the doorway:
Baby Maisie just smiled, took her first steps,
has a fever. He shouts he'll just finish
this patch, mulch these leaves, tighten
the mower's handle. Their lawn is large:
by the time he's clipped one corner,
the far end needs a trim, and before
he knows it, his blades chew through years
of grass. He's come to know the lawn
in sections: the Grumpy Hinterlands
to the north, where pear roots snarl the soil;
the Doldrums, that easy (but boring) flat
stretch to the east; and Graceland
(his favorite), which moats the house, where he
can watch his wife through the windows,
sweeping or reading to Maisie.
                              It is for them
that he mows, and on summer mornings
they spread a blanket and talk—his wife offers
iced tea when he labors by, scrunching
against the sun.

                    Maisie sprouts from a plump
dinner roll of a baby into a fairy child,
an elbowy young lady, a woman. She packs
a car and drives off. Walter curses the brio
of grass that keeps him from loading her bags.

One Sunday, she appears, crosses the lawn
to him, says she's bringing someone home—
a man, she calls him, and Walter twinges
in his knees and hips. *The lawn will be perfect*,
he promises, dizzy in the sunscorch
(for a moment she becomes her mother—
taller, though, darker-haired), and she nods,
turns toward the house (they're in Graceland,

but he can't see inside as well as he could;
he squints—is that his wife by the window?).

Maybe, says Maisie, *you could come in
for dinner tonight.* He sees a shadow,
but it might be a curtain. *Mom's roasting
a duck*, she says. *She's baking a cherry tart.*
He pivots at the lawn's edge and Maisie
matches his steps as he clips toward
the Doldrums (a mixed bag, that section:
easiest but the most boring).
                              Think about it, Dad?
says Maisie, and he turns to see the back
of her head blur away from him, merge
with the dark smudge that was once his house,
though how she gets inside, he can't tell—
it's been ages since he could decipher
the outline of its doors.

On Fading

Years later, Simon wakes
                to a hand like chalk.
He lurches to the bathroom mirror—face
drained of color, head so pale he can see
the towel rack behind him.
                Blank as a window.
Blank as an unnamed street. He inches open
his robe. Blank
            all the way down.
           Well, he thinks. Well.

He showers and dresses, walks to the park
and sits on an empty bench.
            Light and shade play
variations on green all morning, the sky belts

its lusty blue contralto—
              how has he never noticed
before? Even the garbage sparks
            with vibrancy—
grime-caked bottle caps, red paper cups.

He crosses his legs and wonders what kind
of full-color world condones
           a thing like fading,
wonders how he lived
           so long without remarking

on it, wonders why his can't be
           the sort of god to crouch
by the bench, look into his eyes,
             and repaint him.

Second Puberty

It starts the day Linda turns fifty:
she reads the paper without glasses,
pokes like a ship's wheel from her cuffs,
lifts the neighbor's lab from her garden
with ease. At night, her bones ache, and each
morning the furniture seems smaller,
her joints sleeker, her skin more pliant.
She hardly needs coffee.

      Just when she's sold
her house and bought a sailboat for the trip
she thought she'd never take, a phone call:
her mother fell in the kitchen, fractured a hip.
Needs help on the stairs, in the tub.

      What a blessing,
says the nurse, neck screwed to watch
Linda duck into the private room.
Help with all your earthly matters.
Her mother nods. The air hangs stale
and bleached. Linda drives them
to her mother's house, carries the woman
to her bathroom. Eases off her diaper.
Draws her a bath.
      You're my savior, Lin,

her mother says, raising her arms so Linda
can wash beneath them—a church gesture,
from when the congregation says,

      We lift them
      to the Lord,

meaning their hearts, or what their hands
hold of their hearts, meaning blood. Meaning
life. Linda knuckles hair from her forehead,

catches her image in the steam-blurred
window: her giant double knelt at the doubled
tub, a ghost mother bathing her ghost child
before bed. And past them, the reflected
door—she can almost believe the ghosts'
whole house lies behind it, a house
where people fit neatly in their chairs,
where death comes matter-of-factly, without
preamble, and at funerals women
console each other with biscuits so light
they all but melt on the tongue.

Trespassing

The host of fireflies throbs
like a city's lit windows,
so buttery bright you trust,
for a minute, that brick walls
prong among them—but the man
beside you sees only a field:
tiny lights, not distant,

and between them gaps. He hooks
an arm around your waist and chunks
you to him, to his blunt smell
of soaped skin and bourbon
and you long for the city
in your nose and gut. In the domes
of your feet you long for it,

in your shoulders, your thighbones,
for the families met in its rooms
to eat, for the sort of man
who could believe in its streets,
who could see that nothing is more
beautiful and heartbreaking

than a lit window seen from outside.
That man would not ask you to lie
beside him in the dirt, would not
sprout a score of roving hands.
On every side, the field
smolders, but not with lamps kept on
for your arrival. Not hearth flames
or evening newscasts. Insects.
Hoping to mate.
              Humid tonight
but the air burns and burns.
No matter how you branch
your legs beneath him,
it will not consume you.

Dead End

Except now you see it: the vein lattice
surfaced on her hands, the eyes bright
above her crease-mapped cheeks—
every inch of her plotting a place
that could have made you happy.

How many times did she circumnavigate
your cuffs with a needle, guide chicken
to your plate? You can't even brew
coffee—you slop water down the edge,
dust the floor with grounds.

From the counter stool, her sister says,
>*She's tired, Silas. Let her go.*
>With her eyes she adds,
>You made her tired,
>you wore her down
>with your blizzards of apathy,
>your acres of silence.

How many nights, hearing her weep
by the sink, did you slink to the garage
when a word would have soothed her?

You couldn't even give her a child.

No wonder she's not fighting. You turn
and climb the stairs, your knees groaning.
>*She's sleeping*, hisses the sister,
>shuffling after you, but you push
the door anyway, stand by the bed.
She pulls in air with the wistfulness
of a mother gazing down the hallway
where her naked children once toddled,
moments before handing her housekey
to the new owners—

                                you say nothing
to wake her, the first kind thing
you've done, and when she slips away
before dawn, you resign yourself
to an old age of blankness,

        a vacant plane where you sit, pain
                radiating from your joints
        until it's gnawed a hole large enough
        to suck you into oblivion.

Annette Is Fraying

What feels like hair turns out to be her unraveling
thumbtip, loose as a cheap hem—she checks

the clock for proof this is a dream. But no.
An ordinary time. At the library, nothing on darning

flesh, so she hides her shabby skin with gloves
and sleeves, feels the bite of fraying take her bones.

The doctor says she's too far gone for grafts,
refers her to a seamstress, but Annette's insurance

does not cover stitchery, hardly covers this visit.
She leaves fringe-palmed, the bill corroding

her purse. She buys crochet hooks on credit, loops
her skin into a handmade-trivet approximation

of itself—warmer than she'd have guessed.
If she could stop worrying long enough,

she might notice that no one here is cut
from cloth as sturdy as she supposed.

On squally days, they dart their eyes and tuck
themselves into coats, accustomed to the type

of wind that can unstitch a body, to the type
of body sewn slack as tailor's tack.

On Empty

No matter what she puts in them,
Lucy's pockets stay empty. No split seams,
no plunking coins, none of the sudden

heartsick lightness of loss—just pure
plain absence. It strikes her purse next,
her fridge, bookshelves, closet. Cupboards

bare of bowls, shoetrees blank as skeletons.
One day, she lifts her key and no notch
awaits it, no knob, no trace of a door.

She turns and trickles down the stairs,
wafts outside, turns toward the lake but lifts
inland with the wind. She feels vastly wide,

as if she's been unstitched into oxygen,
carbon, hydrogen, nitrogen—even
barium and nickel. Even gold.

She condenses against a beer stein, descends it
to a sticky bar, gusts through a diner's
door while its patrons hunch in sweaters.

When a match strikes near her, she peels apart
to feed it, then twines away. She and her
pockets remain empty, insofar as

she and her pockets remain—as a hole
remains, in some state she does not grasp,
cannot state, in which she will not remain.

Her remains will not grasp pockets.
They will not remain whole—she has become
the pockets now. She is the empty.

Carl's Life Flashes before His Tongue

The morning he dies, Carl empties
the dishwasher while Joan sleeps. Maybe
he'll fry an egg (his mouth waters)—but no,
she'd smell it. He doesn't want a fight.

He'll sugar his bran flakes, take his walk,
and when they meet Ben on Wednesday, order
a filet. She won't scold if Ben's there. Nesting

forks, he feels breathless, as he has more
and more since sixty, and thinks he'll lie
on the couch before eating. A sleep undertow
grips him—just when he's wrenched down,

he sees what's happening, wants to tell Joan
how it feels, but when he tries, the taste
of chalk breaks over him—decades erasing

every word he scrawled, fingers always
coated.
        The taste of snow breaks over him,
he hopes   Ben   meets someone, hopes
Joan remembers

the taxes. He hears her stir and half
                                wants her
to sleep longer   so it's not real
and half wants her here, now,
                hand on his cheek,

her phone voice calling for help   he
hopes she doesn't
take a shower right off   comes for
coffee,
Joan, Joan,   Joan, he tries to say but
the taste

                    of stamps breaks over him,
Congratulations you're invited thank you sorry
for your
            loss.   Taste of
church wine.

Forgive me, Father.   The taste of skin.

Taste of lipstick, whiskey, toothpaste, mints, of
                    waking

sore-necked on the couch   of three
months chicken

            of soccer whistle
                        of eggnog of Joan
                    again and for always.

Clove oil. Seawater. Tobacco. The taste of
steamed

            dishwasher soap breaks over him he
tries to spit
it out   unhooks his lips   it spills
Joan walks in
            they're gone   the tastes
What's wrong

the phone   Honey, talk to me   the
tastes gone   He's not
responding   Carl   his tongue a
blank
chalkboard   Don't leave me

                        his mouth

www.ingramcontent.com/pod-product-compliance
Lightning Source LLC
Chambersburg PA
CBHW071758080526
44588CB00013B/2294